KU-313-714

Umiskin Press, Ireland

Umiskin Press is a not-for-profit publishing house, publishing commissioned and non-commissioned works, mainly though not exclusively, works of labour history, Labour interest, trade union issues, biography, poetry, cultural and social matters. Umiskin is a townland in Kilcar, County Donegal, birthplace of the McGinleys.

Dr Kieran Jack McGinley is the Principal of Umiskin Press having previously been Chairman of Watchword Ltd and is the immediate past President of the ILHS 2014-September 2020.

Umiskin's recent publications were three volumes of Left Lives in Twentieth Century Ireland co-edited by Francis Devine & McGinley(Vol 1+2 ; Devine & Patrick Smylie (Volume 3-April 2020);Mike Mecham's William Walker, Social Activist & Belfast Labourist (1870-1918)October 2019; Devine & Sean Byers: William Walker Centenary Essays (2018); John P Swift Brendan Scott: The Struggle for a Socialist and Secular Ireland December 2020.

Umiskin Press publishes limited editions of hardback and paperback volumes of between 150 and 500 per print run.

How Railwaymen and Dockers defied an Empire
The Irish Munitions Embargo of 1920

Peter Rigney

Contents

Railwaymen defied an empire

A survivor tells how a handful of men made a brave stand for Irish freedom.

By Martin O'Sullivan

IN the late spring of 1920 Ireland was full of British troops, in full war equipment, in training for some punitive expedition or extensive raid, and at that period, and in connection with these expeditions, it was only necessary for the British military authorities to take up a phone and order a troop train to any part of the country.

Immediately after receipt of the order, the Locomotive department in the first instance, would place a first class Locomotive and a senior driver and fireman and the best class coal to work the train, the Traffic Department would provide an experienced guard, and the troop train would get priority over all other trains on the Company's system. However the British military authorities got a most serious shock and setback in the first week of June, 1920.

On Thursday, May 5th, a train arrived at Castlebar Station, County Mayo, with driver H. Blaney in charge, when the train was ready to leave for Westport, a large number of British Troops with an officer in charge boarded the train, but the driver, Mr. Harry Blaney, refused to start. After a conversation with the station authorities the officer approached the footplate of the engine and asked the driver why he refused to start his train, and he was told that he would not start the train while there was a single British soldier or equipment on board.

At this point the officer told him that his refusal could involve him in very serious consequences, in fact, he could be shot, but the driver still refused unless he ordered his men to leave the train, and then the officer looked back and found that his men, who had by now become restive, were engaged in scuffles with the station authorities and the guard who were trying to protect the train.

The officer marched quickly down to his men and ordered them to stop and the driver now took advantage of the officer having to go from him to quell the disturbance. He uncoupled the engine and started off full speed for Westport, having defied and baffled the officer and his men. On arrival at Westport, Blaney was immediately dismissed from the Company's service as the circumstances had to be wired to Railway Headquarters. But Blaney's courageous and unflinching stand at Castlebar prevented British soldiers from travelling on Irish trains. Not a single British soldier has travelled as a matter of fact since that day 46 years ago.

That was surely a magnificent achievement by unarmed men. The example set at Castlebar was followed and upheld by every driver who had British military boarding his train. They risked their lives and lost their jobs. They had also to go through that ordeal on their own.

Dismissal

After the refusal to work trains with British military personnel on board the railway directors issued an infamous order which read: "instant dismissal and on the spot." The drivers who defied the British authorities had to a great extent right on their side because according to railway rules no armed men, military or otherwise, are allowed to travel on the railways. In connection with the statement made here earlier that the drivers had to go through the ordeal on their own it is necessary to put the matter and relevant facts in proper perspective:

The train arrives at the station.

The station master is now in charge and when he sees that the train is ready to leave he instructs the guard to give the right away signal to the driver but in this case the driver has seen British military boarding his train and refuses to start, so the whole responsibility for the non-starting of the train is placed on the driver.

The courageous and unflinching stand of the drivers practically immobilised the thousands of British troops because there was no other form of transport in the country at that period. One could go from one end of the country to the other and would not see a mechanically-propelled vehicle anywhere.

Important

The refusal to carry the troops was surely of paramount importance to the gallant band of men who were actually using force against the British Government in the struggle for independence. And many high-ranking officers of the I.R.A. have stated that the action of the Irish locomotive drivers in preventing the transport of British troops on their punitive raids was certainly the very greatest help that they could have got.

The action of those men was called "The Munitions Strike of 1920," but it was not a strike in the proper sense of the word because the drivers had failed to get the unions support which in the circumstances was not surprising as the Railmen's Union at that time was British-controlled and British-based and the rules would not allow any such move. So they had to face the ordeal of a prolonged and bitter strike without any strike pay.

After about a fortnight a collection was taken from all the railway employes which continued all through the duration of the strike, of 1/- per week. Some time after this the general public were asked to contribute and about £100 was collected in all. The strike lasted for about six months, and in the closing stages at least 50 per cent. of the employes had been dismissed.

Only married men were considered for those collections. While I was employed I was entrusted to bring sums of money to drivers who were dismissed. As far as I can recollect, the amount to each man never exceeded 50/-. It may have been increased at some later date, but I have no knowledge of it; anyhow I was dismissed myself and as I had to go back to my native town I was more or less out of touch.

TOMORROW: How I was involved . . . and dismissed.

> *We can defeat them by ... our will and wit against their numbers and material power.*

The first time I ever heard of the munitions strike of 1920 was when watching Ken Loach's film, the Wind that Shakes the Barley, when the locomotive driver character, played by Liam Cunningham was beaten up by British soldiers when he refused to work a train.

The Munitions Strike as it is known or more correctly the Arms Embargo marks the commencement of a difficult period for railway history within the decade of centenaries. It was a period that led to division, violence and hurt that lived on well passed the end of the Civil War and the foundation of the new state, not just in the railway, but in our nation as a whole.

In reading this extremely informative booklet, I am struck by the fact that railwaymen and Dockers were inspired to undertake this course of action because of action taken by workers in London in protest at Britain's involvement in the Russo-Polish conflict. In 1920 communication was not as easy as it is now and levels of formal education would also have been much lower, but despite this workers in Ireland learned of what was happening in London and undertook a course of action, because they believed what was happening in Ireland at the time was wrong and they stood up for those beliefs, despite the enormous personal cost to themselves and their families.

I also found the vivid accounts from the witness statements captured by the Bureau of Military History fascinating and they gave a real insight into the dilemma that faced many of these workers.

I commend Railway Historian, Peter Rigney for the detailed research he has undertaken to produce this booklet and hope that many will benefit from learning about this period of our history.

Jim Meade

Chief Executive

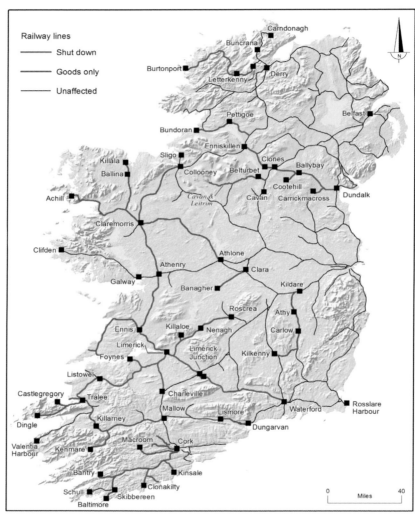

Railway lines

— Shut down

— Goods only

— Unaffected

Map of lines affected by the Munitions Strike

Acknowledgements

The railways have been in existence in Ireland since 1834 and been part of social, economic and political developments throughout that period. Iarnród Éireann has always had a very proactive approach to its heritage, whether it be archives, historical buildings or heritage vehicles. I was therefore honoured when approached to assist in their contribution to the Decade of Centenaries.

I am very grateful to Jane Cregan of Corporate Communications, Iarnród Éireann for her support in making this publication possible. Thanks are due to the Committee of the Irish Railway Record Society for access to the railway company archives and to their photographic collection. Thanks to Jack McGinley of Umiskin Press. A debt of gratitude is owed to Shay Cody, Ciarán Cooney, Brian Hanley, Lar Joye, Martin Maguire, Mike Murphy, Mary McMillen, Gerry Mooney, Eve Morrison, Mary Muldowney, Hassard Stacpoole, Donal O'Drisceoil and Pádraig Yeates. Thanks are also due to University College Cork for the map and to Independent News & Media for Martin O' Sullivan's article.

I first took an interest in this strike when a student at Trinity forty years ago. The memory of the Munitions Strike was still very much alive as were some of the participants. I spoke at that time to many railwaymen whose fathers had been dismissed. One Athlone driver that I spoke to remarked to me that he regretted not asking his father more about it. Apart from family reminiscences we get our history from books and this is where another driver from Athlone, Martin O'Sullivan comes into the story. He was involved in the strike and in 1967 wrote an article on it for the Irish Independent. This was forty seven years after the strike and it had still not made its way into the history books. He wrote 'It is almost impossible to believe that those important events where not recorded in any recent history of Ireland in the years 1920 and onwards to the present day'. Since then the published work of Charles Townshend, Pádraig Yeates and Conor McCabe has increased our understanding of the strike.

In this Decade of Commemorations it is only fitting that the contribution of ordinary railwaymen and dockers to the Independence Struggle is recognised by this pamphlet.

Peter Rigney

ASLEF	Associated Society of Locomotive Engineers and Firemen
BMH	Bureau of Military History: A collection of statements taken in the forties and fifties from people with experience of the 1913 to 1921 period
DSER	Dublin and South Eastern Railway
GNR	Great Northern Railway
GWR	Great Western Railway of England. Operators of Rosslare port
GS&WR	Great Southern and Western Railway
ILP&TUC	Irish Labour Party and Trade Union Congress, often known simply as Congress
LNWR	London and North Western Railway, operator of North Wall cross channel steamers
ITGWU	Irish Transport and General Workers' Union
MGWR	Midland Great Western Railway
MSP	Military Service Pension Application for service between 1916 and 1923
NUR	National Union of Railwaymen

The Cast

Frank Brooke	Chairman of the DSER. Member of the Irish Privy Council.
Robert Crawford	Company Secretary GS&WR.
E. A. Neale	Manager of the GS&WR and Reserve Army Officer.
Sir Eric Geddes	Minister for Transport, former manager of North Eastern Railway of England, brother of the British Ambassador to the USA.
G.T. Glover	Locomotive Engineer of the GNR.
Hamar Greenwood	Chief Secretary of State for Ireland.
M.F. Keogh	Manager of the MGWR.
Mark Sturgis	Civil Servant in Dublin Castle and Assistant to John Anderson.
Jim Slattery	Member of Collins 'Squad' who shot Frank Brooke in July 1920.
James Thomas MP	Former locomotive driver and General Secretary of the NUR.

The ships

Anna Dorette Boog.   London   1767 tons.
Owners Dorea & Co., London.

Jolly George   Liverpool   1328 tons.
Owners Entente Steamship Co. London.

Polberg   London.   1343 tons.
Owners British & Irish Steam Packet Co. Dublin.

Slievemore   Belfast.   1053 tons.
Owners London & North Western Railway.

Source: *Mercantile Navy list and Maritime Directory 1920*

In May 1920 the biggest campaign of civil resistance against the British Empire in Ireland began when Irish railwaymen and dockers refused to transport armed troops, armed police or war materials. It was initiated by two veterans of the 1916 Rising, lasted seven months and involved the dismissal of approximately one thousand railwaymen and hundreds of dockers.[1] This is a story of politically motivated, largely non-violent, industrial action on a massive scale. While the British presented the separatist campaign in Ireland as the work of paid assassins, they termed a 'murder gang', the actions of ordinary workers demonstrated that the independence movement in Ireland had widespread popular support. General Sir Neville Macready, Commander of the Army in Ireland, described the strike as 'a serious setback to British military actions in Ireland'.[2]

In 1967 Martin O'Sullivan, a retired locomotive driver and Munitions Strike participant, wrote an article for the *Irish Independent*, in which he asked why so little attention had been paid to the strike by historians.[3] It was to be another twelve years before the first academic study of the strike appeared, by British historian Charles Townshend; he expressed surprise that Irish historians had paid very little attention to this 'politically motivated industrial action'.[4]

Irish railways had been under state control since December 1916 as a wartime emergency measure. Ownership remained with the shareholders but the Ministry of Transport controlled the operation of the railways. The takeover agreement guaranteed compensation payments to the companies. This guarantee was to come back and bite the British during the Munitions Strike.

The largest company was the Great Southern and Western Railway (GS&WR), which ran from Dublin to Cork, Kerry and Waterford, and operated about one third of the railway network. The second largest company was the Great Northern Railway, which had two thirds of its network in Ulster. The Midland Great Western Railway (MGWR) ran from Dublin to Galway, Mayo and Sligo. The Dublin and South Eastern Railway (DSER) ran between Dublin, Wexford and Waterford.

There was an overlap between heads of the railways and the Irish political establishment. Sir William Goulding, Chairman of the GS&WR, was an Irish Privy Councillor, spokesman for the Irish companies and a pillar of the southern unionist community. His brother Edward was an influential Conservative MP. Similarly, the Chairman of the DSER Frank Brooke, was also a member of the Irish Privy Council and a close friend of the Viceroy.

By spring 1920, much of Ireland outside of Ulster was slipping out of British control. The Dublin Castle administration was in a shambles. Warren Fisher, head of the British Civil Service stated: 'The government of Ireland strikes me as woodenly stupid and almost devoid of imagination'.[5] Neville Macready took over command of the army in Ireland in March. Not a man to mince his words, he damned the administration in Dublin Castle in the following terms: 'Before I had been (there) for three hours I was honestly flabbergasted at the administrative chaos that seemed to reign there'.[6] His views on Dublin Castle were nothing to his views on Ireland and its people: 'I loathe the country...and its people with a depth deeper than the sea and more violent than that which I feel against the Germans'.[7] The top level of the civil service underwent a complete change and a new small team of senior civil servants was put in place. Hamar Greenwood was appointed to the Cabinet as Chief Secretary in April 1920. Sir John Anderson was drafted in as Under Secretary and his team included Andy Cope, who was to become an intermediary between Sinn Féin and the British in peace efforts and Mark Sturgis, a former tax official whose diary gives a candid insight into the British response to the strike. In August Anderson's team had to move, for safety reasons, inside the walls of Dublin Castle.[8]

The Royal Irish Constabulary was being weakened by resignations and by attacks on barracks. In the first four months of 1920, 219 barracks had been destroyed and 21 tax offices burnt down.[9] Tax collectors were attacked, sometimes shot, and their records either stolen or destroyed. In an attempt to bring the RIC up to strength, the British recruited ex-soldiers, who soon become known as the Black and Tans, to the RIC. Meanwhile Dáil Éireann was establishing Departments of State and a network of courts which were displacing the established court system. By August the British acknowledged that their grip on Ireland was loosening and 'in the south and west many unionists were embracing, however, reluctantly, the new ideas and were not unwilling to make use of the Sinn Féin Courts'.[10] Curfews were imposed on parts of Ireland in an attempt to regain control but the legitimacy of the British state was slipping away. At the same time,

Britain was faced with problems of Imperial overstretch. The victors of the war were busy taking over territories previously controlled by the Ottoman Empire and the former German colonies in Africa. Britain sought to control Mesopotamia (Iraq), Persia (Iran) and Egypt, amongst other countries. Occupation duties in Germany and the need to have troops available at home to deal with industrial disputes were also soaking up military manpower.

'Hands off Russia'

There was widespread fear in Britain that Winston Churchill's desire to bring down the new Russian Soviet state would drag Britain into the Russian-Polish conflict and the Russian Civil War. A Home Office intelligence report stated:

> Never have we known such excitement and antagonism to be around against any project as has been around amongst the workers by the possibility of war with Russia. On every hand ex-serviceman are saying that they will never take part in any war again. [11]

On 13 May 1920, the cargo ship, the *SS Jolly George* was in London docks waiting to be loaded with munitions for Poland. The dockers refused to load this ship as part of what became known as the 'Hands Off Russia' campaign. Ernest Bevin, their union official gave immediate support, justifying it later by saying:

> Whatever may be the merits or demerits of the theory of government in Russia, that is a matter for Russia, and we have no right to determine their form of government any more than we would tolerate Russia determining our form of government. [12]

This view was echoed some days later by J.H. Thomas, General Secretary of the National Union of Railwaymen. (NUR) A former locomotive driver, he became Labour MP for Derby in 1910, General Secretary of the NUR in 1916, and a Privy Councillor in 1917. He accused the Government of drawing Britain into a new war in Europe behind the back of parliament, stating that his union had decided to instruct its members 'not to load, carry or help in the conveyance of munitions'. [13] It was not, however, Thomas' intention that this would apply to Ireland.

The first Irish hunger striker in 1920 was the prominent trade unionist, William O'Brien, General Treasurer of ITGWU and a key player in the story of the striking dockers and railwaymen. Arrested in Dublin in March 1920, he was transported to England and imprisoned, without charge, in Wormwood Scrubs Jail. Protesting against his illegal incarceration, he went on hunger strike on 18 March and thanks to a campaign by Labour MPs and trade union colleagues he was released on 6 May. While in jail he had taken a keen interest in the *Jolly George* dispute. In an interview with the *Freeman's Journal* O'Brien remarked:

> We see that the London dockers have taken action to save the Russian Workers' Republic, and who knows that they may soon realize that they have an even more pressing duty nearer home.[14]

On 5 April 1920, IRA prisoners in Mountjoy Jail went on hunger strike demanding prisoner of war status. A week into the strike the Irish Labour Party & Trades Union Congress, hereafter referred to as Congress, organised a general strike in support of them. It was a resounding success, lasted two days, 13 and 14 April, and secured the release of the prisoners. Tom Johnson, Secretary of Congress, described the event as: 'an example to the world of how labour might make its will effective – an example of solidarity without parallel.'[15] Immediately before the strike Congress had issued an open letter to British workers, seeking support for the hunger strikers. Of the eighteen signatories, nine were railwaymen, pointing to a high level of politicisation among railway workers which would be significant in the forthcoming Munitions Strike.[16]

The Beginning of the Munitions Strike

Two 1916 veterans played a key role in starting the strike. Michael Donnelly was a member of the Irish Citizen Army and a deep sea docker, while Christopher Moran had been a member of the Irish Volunteers and was a porter on the DSER. Deep sea dockers were employed on a casual basis and were members of the ITGWU. On 20 May, Donnelly walked into Liberty Hall, headquarters of the ITGWU, and told William O'Brien about a shipload of military lorries waiting to be unloaded at the North Wall.[17] It was agreed that dockers would refuse to unload the ship and refuse all cooperation with the Army should they unload it.[18] As a result of this action the SS *Anna Dorette Boog* had to have its cargo of lorries unloaded by members of the Royal Engineers.

Bored soldiers 'glued to the ground'

Cross channel dockers on the other hand, were employed full time by shipowners such as the London and North Western Railway (LNWR). These workers refused to handle guns bound for the Dublin Metropolitan Police and within days 400 dockers, members of the NUR, were on strike. The *Irish Independent* reported that:

> Pickets continue active at North Wall. The TSS *Slievemore*, which brought over a tin case of revolvers consigned to the Dublin Metropolitan Police which the NUR refused to handle, and which thus initiated the trouble still lies at the sheds, the balance of the cargo still untouched. [19]

North Wall dockers remained on strike for the next seven months and were joined by 150 dockers in Rosslare Harbour, employed by the Great Western Railway of England who were also members of the NUR. Despite the fact

> *I loathe the country
> ... and its people
> with a depth deeper
> than the sea and
> more violent than
> which I feel against
> the Germans.*

that the strike originated on the docks it is seen as a railway affair because the railwaymen's refusal to transport armed soldiers, policemen or munitions severely hindered the movement of the British Army around Ireland. Port facilities were open to all ships and the military was free to berth and unload them using military labour. Railwaymen were not, however, as easily replaced by soldiers as dockers.

The Strike Spreads to the Railways

A few days after the action at the North Wall, another ship carrying military equipment docked at Kingstown (Dun Laoghaire) at the Admiralty Wharf. Its cargo was unloaded into railway wagons by soldiers, but railway workers then refused to work the train. Christopher Moran, a porter in Westland Row station in his witness statement to The Bureau of Military History, [20] describes how on Sunday 23 May:

> A British gun boat, the SS *Polberg* [21] arrived in Dun Laoghaire with a load of munitions for the British army in Ireland and berthed at the admiralty pier. Twenty-two wagons were despatched by the DSER to Kingstown to be loaded up with this material which was duly done. I was on Sunday morning work and the then stationmaster at Westland Row, a Mr. Ryan, ordered me to go down to Kingstown with an engine and bring the wagons of munitions over to Kingsbridge and hand them over to the GS&WR.
>
> Before doing anything, I went…to mass and on my way to the chapel, I passed two of our railwaymen who were having a talk on the sidewalk. They did not know me. As I passed, I heard them say to one another, that if they were instructed or ordered to go, they would not do so. I presumed they were referring to the wagons of munitions at Kingstown. At this time, the British had landed troops in Russia,

to fight the Bolsheviks or communists there, and the British dockers refused to load munition for this expeditionary force. I began to think that if the British dockers refused to handle munitions for their troops to kill Russians, why should I handle munitions for British forces to kill my own countrymen. When I got back to the station, I informed Mr. Ryan that I would not go to Kingstown for the wagons. An ex British army man named Burgess was now detailed to go, but he refused also, as did every other man who was approached.

I now got on my bicycle and proceeded to the headquarters of the National Union of Railwaymen to report what had happened. On crossing Mount Street, I met an engine driver who was off duty named Frank Shields. I told him what had happened, and he agreed also that, if he was detailed, he would refuse to go. I cycled on to Lansdowne cottages and there I contacted the secretary of our (union) branch, John Noctor and told him what had happened, and he said he would back me to the last.

The munitions never were taken from Kingstown by rail. I understand that they were reloaded on the boat, which put to sea again. The traffic manager at Westland Row - George Mc Donald – interviewed me and asked me for my reason for refusing to take the train. My reply to him was that, when Englishmen were refusing to handle munitions to kill Russians, I would not handle munitions to kill Irishmen. He said, 'this is very serious, and it is hard to see the end of it. I then said, 'I am sorry sir, but I don't think there is any end to it. I was not dismissed, or ever asked to handle munitions again.'[22]

Why did Moran escape disciplinary action? The answer to this question lies in the decision taken in March to terminate war time price controls on food. This provoked a political crisis amidst fears of food shortages and soaring prices. Dockers and railway workers in a number of locations refused to handle food exports. In an attempt to defuse the situation, the British Government advised the railway companies not to take any action which might provoke a railway strike, 'in view of the difficult situation which already exists in Ireland'.[23] Moran was a beneficiary of this advice.

The articles not to be handled were guns, ammunition for guns, bayonets, bombs, aeroplanes, and such things obviously designed for the purpose of destroying life—that is, killing materials of all kinds. They did not refuse to transport soldiers. They would do so 'provided the objectionable material had been removed'.[24]

The Munitions Strike escalated when Great Southern & Western Railway (GS&WR) staff at Cork and Kingsbridge refused to accept consignments of rifles which had been delivered to the station by soldiers. Again, no disciplinary action was taken and the General Manager informed the board that this was in compliance with the Ministry of Transport advice to avoid a railway strike.[25] On 1 June ten chests of guns were delivered to Newbridge Station. The guard on the passenger train refused to take them stating that 'he had instructions from his society not to do so'. The following day, a special train to take two officers and 31 men from Kildare to Portarlington failed to run when the driver refused to take the train. No disciplinary action was taken against any of these men.[26]

Access to the railway system was an essential element of the Army's mobility. According to the Cabinet minutes of 31 May, Hamar Greenwood expressed hope that the rebellion could be suppressed by the mobile columns then being planned by Macready. The notes of the meeting taken by Tom Jones (Lloyd George's private secretary) showed considerably less optimism.[27] Greenwood had in fact told the cabinet: 'Our forces are still glued to the ground and we cannot succeed until our mobility is greater than theirs'. Macready concurred stating: 'The troops are now stationary except the cavalry. The War Office is fulfilling my demands as fast as they can but they are held up by the strike'.[28]

Compounding the transport problem faced by the British was the state of their motor fleet. In March 1920 the army in Ireland had only 156 lorries at its disposal. A further 319 were delivered before the end of the year. Vehicle reliability was another problem. The Army *Record of the Rebellion* described how:

> The Disposals Board seem to have sold off all the best vehicles and to have retained those which were nearly worn out or deficient in … spare parts…Those were bad days in 1920 and the inefficiency of motorised transport was a cause of daily complaints.[29]

The NUR was placed in an awkward position by the action of its Irish members. There was a difference between industrial action against an unpopular war in distant Eastern Europe and industrial action which directly undermined Government authority in what was still part of the United Kingdom. The directive on handling of munitions to Poland was withdrawn, with the *Railway Gazette* editorial writer wondering how a union could 'declare a revolutionary policy on 23 May and withdraw it on June 2'.[30] The NUR recognised this U-turn as a source of embarrassment:

> *I began to think that if the British dockers refused to handle munitions for their troops to kill Russians, why should I handle munitions for British forces to kill my own countrymen.*

> Our executive council let their sympathies rule them and not their reason. They passed a resolution in favour of the policy over the *Jolly George* …and when they found it impossible to carry it out, they had to modify it.[31]

British railway companies were seeking to reverse many of the wage increases and improvements in conditions which the unions had secured during the period of Government war time control and the NUR needed the goodwill of the Government in these negotiations. Faced with this dilemma, J.H. Thomas telegraphed the Irish office of the union urging the men to resume normal working to allow the British Labour movement to act on their behalf. He announced the convening of a special conference in Bristol of Irish branches to discuss the 'Irish question'.[32] However, Irish members of the NUR refused his request to resume normal working and their action continued for another six months.

The conference was attended by 70 delegates from all over Ireland who were described as:

Men with souls embittered by their experience, self-confident, strong-willed, and powerful in their convictions

> *I got on my bicycle and proceeded to the headquarters of the National Union of Railwaymen to report what had happened.*

politically in opposition to them, striving to find a way out of the difficulty in which their brother Trade Unionists had found themselves. [33]

Contrasting views among union members can be seen in the cases of two GNR firemen. One veteran of the Battle of Jutland said: 'I have no sympathy with the political movement and refused entirely on the grounds of fear. I was in the navy for three years and four months and regret having to take the step of refusing.' Another GNR fireman who volunteered for army service in 1915, had served five years abroad and was recommended for the Distinguished Conduct Medal. He refused to work a train in Belfast on principle. [34]

The conference passed three motions, which managed to maintain a semblance of unity among the Irish membership. Motion one congratulated the executive in trying to find a solution to the whole Irish question; motion two stated that the situation in Ireland was due to the failure to govern the country in accordance with the wishes of its people, urged the cessation of 'outrage' and called on the Government to prevent provocation by the sending of munitions to Ireland. The third motion agreed to seek a meeting with the Prime Minister to promote solutions based on the motion above. [35]

Dismissals

While the Bristol conference maintained a façade of unity in the NUR in Ireland, the outcome fell short of providing the resolution which many had hoped for. Railway workers continued to refuse to transport armed men or munitions. Eric Geddes, Minister for Transport, reported to the Cabinet that a letter had been issued to the companies on 10 June stating that men who refused to handle military traffic should be dealt with under the disciplinary procedures. What Geddes did not report was that Ministry officials had twice verbally advised the companies to defer any action until after the Bristol conference.[36] Dismissals began around 20 June, and by 25 June the GS&WR Board was advised that almost sixty men had been dismissed. Trains in the Limerick district had almost ceased to run, Tralee was little better and the line between Limerick and Waterford would shortly close to passenger traffic. By 15 July the GS&WR had dismissed 270 men for refusals and laid off a further 150 in Rosslare Harbour and Limerick. The number of dismissals continued to grow, and by the end of the month the GS&WR had dismissed 357 traffic and 253 loco staff, roughly ten per cent of the total employees in each department.[37] By the end of the strike over 1000 railwaymen and 500 dockers had been dismissed or suspended.

As the strike was 'unofficial' for both the NUR and ASLEF, Congress took over the running of the dispute. On 9 June it asked Trades Councils to build a broad front by forming local committees to organise collections, involving trade unionists together with sympathisers and supporters from outside the trade union ranks as the sacrifices made by the dockers was 'for the people of Ireland as a whole' and dockers had already sacrificed £5000 in lost wages. While the fund was launched in support of the 400 North Wall dockers, it eventually had to support 1,500 dockers and railwaymen. This appeal was successful and the fund raised a total of £117,510 during the course of the dispute.[38] This is calculated to be circa £5.2 million in today's money.[39] The Dáil Ministry of Labour gave £1500 towards the strike in June.[40] William O'Brien also attempted to get access to the remainder of the anti-conscription fund to support the strike but was blocked by John Dillon of the Irish Parliamentary Party, one of the trustees.[41] Michael Collins had hoped to get money from America to support the strike but this never materialized because of acrimony between DeValera and Irish-American organizations, led by the old Fenian John Devoy.

Between late June and mid-July, the companies lobbied the Government for a clear directive on how to handle the situation. Sir William Goulding, Chairman of the GS&WR and spokesman for the Irish railways, wrote to Bonar Law, leader of the Conservative Party, stating that a clear directive would be preferable to the informal 'understandings' given by officials of the Ministry of Transport. He concluded that 'the board are most anxious to carry out the wishes of the Government in any way, if they knew what they are'.[42]

Based on what they knew about the Irish trade union movement the British might well have thought that dismissals would be followed by an immediate railway strike based on the Larkinite slogan 'An injury to one is the concern of all'. Congress chose to go in a diametrically opposite direction for strategic reasons because it considered that Lloyd George and Winston Churchill wanted to provoke social and economic chaos in Ireland by closing the railway system and projecting the blame for this on the railway workers.

> *Our forces are still glued to the ground and we cannot succeed until our mobility is greater than theirs.*

> Tory newspapers and eminent statesmen have been for a week or two talking freely and quite gratuitously of the general railway strike... there has been no talk about a general strike of railwaymen with the ranks of Irish labour...we must not allow ourselves to be provoked into precipitate actions. ...let no man leave his work unless he personally is dismissed.[43]

The British TUC held a special Conference to deal with the Irish question on 13 July. A Miners' Union motion calling for a ballot on a general strike in support of Irish self-determination, was passed together with an NUR amendment advocating a cessation of "outrage" by the Irish side in exchange for a withdrawal of the army of occupation, and the concession of Dominion Home Rule for all of Ireland with protection for minorities. The parliamentary committee of the TUC met Lloyd George the following week, but their views carried little weight as can be seen from the Cabinet meeting of 26 July at which it was decided that the policy of dismissals should be intensified. Sir John Anderson, Assistant Under-Secretary for Ireland set the tone when he said: 'The railway directors and managers had not put their backs into this and ought now to do so. At the present we shall be broken before the railway companies.' [44]

The dispute reached a crisis point in the last week of July, with the political and military authorities taking diametrically opposed actions within a few days of each other. On 27 July, Army Headquarters in Dublin decided that:

> Owing to the state of the country the military authorities do not at present propose normally to use the railways for the transport of arms, ammunition, explosives or motor spirit. [45]

Success for the Munitions Strike seemed to be on the horizon. However, this decision was reversed as soon as it came to the attention of the Cabinet in London.

On 28 July Lloyd George had a meeting with Unionist representatives, led by Sir Edward Carson, at which he threatened the dismissal of all Irish railwaymen.[46] This tougher approach was conveyed by the Ministry of Transport and a circular was issued giving effect to this new policy of mass dismissals and stating that in each case of a refusal to carry passengers or goods, the individual concerned was to be disciplined and the next person on the roster was to be called upon to do the disputed work.[47] This would have led to a cascade of dismissals. However the circular was never implemented due to an intervention from another quarter.

On 29 July Frank Brooke, Chairman of the DSER was sitting in his office in Westland Row station around lunchtime. Paddy Daly and Jim Slattery of the IRA counter-intelligence unit, known as 'The Squad', entered the building; Jim Slattery went into Brooke's office and shot him dead.[48] Brooke had been advocating bringing over detachments of the Royal Engineers to run the trains.[49] The funeral was hardly over when the DSER head office began to receive unsolicited CVs for the vacant seat on the board.[50]

Other railway mangers came to the attention of the Squad during the strike. M. F. Keogh of the MGWR and E.A. Neale of the GS&WR were kept under observation by IRA intelligence, with a view to kidnapping them to try and curb dismissals of railwaymen.[51] According to Lawrence Nugent another (unnamed) railway director approached the IRA through an intermediary, Mrs. Zigmen, a Jewish lady who ran a cigarette shop in Baggot Street and sent a letter asking for mercy saying he was not guilty of spying and denying that he was collaborating with the British.[52]

The shooting of Brooke ended the discussion of the use of Royal Engineers as a substitute labour force. It also altered the trajectory of the companies' response towards the Munitions Strike. Fearing that their policy on carrying Crown forces was about to become a matter of life and death, the GS&WR changed their policy on dismissals, which were no longer automatic but would require board sanction. In response, the Ministry of Transport directed that munition strikers should be disciplined. Goulding, spokesman for the railway companies, responded by stating that they were no longer going to discipline munition strikers. The British policy of mass dismissals was now in ruins. At the Cabinet meeting of 11 August, it was reported that between 900 and 1,000 railwaymen had been dismissed, but that dismissals were now proceeding in a half-hearted manner.[53]

While the companies and the Government were working together up to the Brooke shooting this co-operation unsurprisingly ground to a halt. The Government now needed to coerce the companies into implementing mass dismissals and considered withholding compensation payments under the 1916 takeover agreement. However, the plan hit a snag when the English Attorney General warned that even if the railways were closed, the companies would still be entitled to be paid their full compensation payments and that this issue could not be resolved without an Act of Parliament.[54]

The railway companies were now reluctant to dismiss men without an explicit written instruction from the Ministry of Transport stating that they would dismiss men if told to do so in 'precise and unambiguous terms'. The Ministry replied that they didn't have the legal power to direct company disciplinary procedures.[55] In the light of the Brooke shooting no one wanted to take responsibility for mass dismissals. Breaking ranks, the DSER reinstated suspended men at the end of August. [56]

In late August the *Freeman's Journal* reported that while in the early stages of the dispute all munitions strikers had been dismissed, the railways were now carrying out a new practice of suspension instead of dismissal.

> All the men now are suspended, this being an important technical point for the men, as it preserves the continuity of their contract with their employers and keeps alive their interests in superannuation and other funds to which they belong.[57]

While dismissal is the permanent cessation of an employment contract, suspension implies that the companies believed that the men would be reinstated. It also allowed companies to claim wages of suspended men under the compensation agreement until the Government found out, as the following GNR correspondence shows: 'The Minister of Transport has notified that he will not accept any debit in the shape of wages to the men suspended in connection with the refusals to work government traffic'.[58] It would appear that at least some of the railway companies were claiming back wages which they had not paid. No wonder Mark Sturgis described the company directors as 'a shifty lot concerned only with the maintenance of their subsidies'.[59]

The Effect of the Strike on Train Services

Congress outlined the British tactics:

> The plan adopted by Dublin Castle was to force the issue by sending parties of armed troops and police to board every train no matter in which direction it was going. The armed parties would board the train as passengers. When they were refused the troops would leave the train which would proceed to its destination where the crew member who had refused would be dismissed.[60]

The board was most anxious to carry out the wishes of the Government in any way, if they knew what they are.

The strike put the army in the humiliating position of having to prove to civilians they were unarmed before they would be allowed to travel. In Waterford on 14 June the *Railway Gazette* reported that a party of 28 soldiers were marooned on their way to Kilkenny. The corporal approached the station staff and said the men had not eaten for a considerable time. Following this, half of the group who were unarmed got the train to Kilkenny while the remainder returned to Waterford barracks. There are many other examples of disruptions on the GS&WR with Newbridge being a hotspot for delays because of its

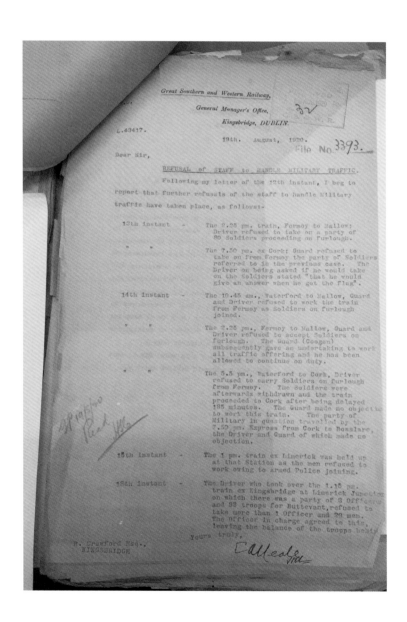

Great Southern and Western Railway,

General Manager's Office,

Kingsbridge, DUBLIN.

L.43417.

19th. August, 1920.

File No. 3393.

Dear Sir,

REFUSAL of STAFF to HANDLE MILITARY TRAFFIC.

Following my letter of the 12th instant, I beg to report that further refusals of the staff to handle Military traffic have taken place, as follows:-

13th instant - The 2.25 pm. train, Fermoy to Mallow; Driver refused to take on a party of 80 Soldiers proceeding on furlough.

" " The 7.50 pm. ex Cork; Guard refused to take on from Fermoy the party of Soldiers referred to in the previous case. The Driver on being asked if he would take on the Soldiers stated "that he would give an answer when he got the flag".

14th instant - The 10.45 am., Waterford to Mallow, Guard and Driver refused to work the train from Fermoy as Soldiers on furlough joined.

" " The 2.25 pm., Fermoy to Mallow, Guard and Driver refused to accept Soldiers on furlough. The Guard (Coogan) subsequently gave an undertaking to work all traffic offering and he has been allowed to continue on duty.

" " The 5.5 pm., Waterford to Cork, Driver refused to carry Soldiers on furlough from Fermoy. The Soldiers were afterwards withdrawn and the train proceeded to Cork after being delayed 185 minutes. The Guard made no objection to work this train. The party of Military in question travelled by the 7.40 pm. Express from Cork to Rosslare, the Driver and Guard of which made no objection.

15th instant - The 1 pm. train ex Limerick was held up at that Station as the men refused to work owing to armed Police joining.

16th instant - The Driver who took over the 1.15 pm. train ex Kingsbridge at Limerick Junction on which there was a party of 3 Officers and 33 troops for Buttevant, refused to take more than 1 Officer and 20 men. The Officer in charge agreed to this, leaving the balance of the troops behind.

Yours truly,

F. Crawford Esq.,
KINGSBRIDGE

proximity to a number of military barracks. In Fermoy a party of 80 soldiers going on leave waited three days before they found a crew that would take them. At Limerick Junction a driver found 3 officers and 88 troops heading for Buttevant and refused to take more than one officer and twenty men. Surprisingly the officer in charge agreed with this and left the balance of the troops behind.[61]

Mayo Sinn Féin activists commandeered cars to get passengers to their destinations when all traffic was stopped west of Castlerea in late June.[62] The *Sligo Champion* of 10 July reported, 'Galway and Mayo are practically isolated, and nobody knows how soon the same may be the fate of Sligo'. The *Southern Star* reported that citizens of Bantry lost all train services from July. Armed RIC had boarded every train scheduled to leave from there. When the railwaymen refused to work the trains they were dismissed, causing the line from Bantry to Drimoleague to be closed due to lack of staff. [63] Other sections of the line remained working, with for example 70 wagons of cattle being transported by train from Skibereen fair in September.[64]

Military freight was an early target of the strikers and one of the earliest incidents on the GS&WR occurred on 8 June when a driver refused to attach two wagons containing aeroplane parts to his train at Lucan. In another incident, in late July, two wagons of military stores in Kingsbridge yard became the focus of attention. Drivers, guards and shunters refused to attach the wagons to a train, causing a chain of 31 dismissals over a few days. Michael Collins instructed that the wagons be burned in order to stop the chain of dismissals. This incident received widespread publicity, not least due to the refusal of the Dublin Fire Brigade to tackle the fire.[65]

The Smaller Railways

Railways were more important in the remoter parts of the south and west due to the poor state of the roads. This was especially the case in Donegal, which was served by two narrow gauge railways, the County Donegal Railways Joint Committee and the Londonderry and Lough Swilly Railway. (LLSR) The two companies had different experiences of the strike. County Donegal Railways operated normally for most of the strike, except for the line from Strabane to Letterkenny which closed during August after trains were fired on and the line was blocked by the IRA. The LLSR was more affected by the strike. By the end of July 39 men had been suspended and few were left to work the remaining restricted service.[66] The line from

Letterkenny to Burtonport closed down completely from late July until August and from November to the end of the strike.[67] This left the British reliant on ships to get troops and supplies into west Donegal. It would also have had implications for people living in isolated areas.

Burning wagons at Kingsbridge

Most of the other narrow-gauge railways had a County Council influence in their management, which presented difficulties for the implementation of British directives, as Sinn Féin controlled most authorities since the local elections in 1920. The British army complained that train crews on the Tralee and Dingle railway who refused to handle military traffic faced no sanction which is not surprising as the stationmasters in Tralee and Dingle were both IRA intelligence officers.[68]

The Cavan and Leitrim Railway is a case study in how a line totally unaffected by the dispute was deliberately drawn in by the military. From November military parties began to turn up at Mohill and were refused transport, following which the crews were summarily dismissed. A shortage of crews caused the suspension of all services. While the general manager 'hoped to run the occasional food train', even this proved impossible as on 10 December the Ministry ordered that the line be closed.[69] This desire to run occasional food trains highlights the role of the railway system in food distribution, particularly in remote areas.

On 3 July the *Sligo Champion* described a delay on the Sligo to Enniskillen train when the crew refused to start when a party of the Cornwall Regiment boarded. Only when an officer guaranteed that no ammunition was being carried did 'The train steam out taking the (h)armless warriors with it amid the cheers of a large crowd'.

Previous service in the Great War did not deter railwaymen from supporting the Munitions Strike. A significant number of railwaymen had returned to their jobs after war time service and in addition a large number of railway staff were recruited to new vacancies created by the introduction of the eight hour day in February 1919, with companies favouring the recruitment of former soldiers.[70] When Christopher Moran refused to go to Kingstown to collect the wagons of munitions, the next man to refuse was an ex-soldier named Burgess. In Cavan station two porters, both ex-soldiers, and a foreman were dismissed for refusing to handle barbed wire and steel shutters.[71]

Intimidation

Charles Townshend has observed that many of the incidents of intimidation during the strike were akin to what could be expected in a 'normal' trade dispute.[72] Twenty one incidents of intimidation by the IRA were identified between June and October 1920, the majority on the GNR.[73] Goulding described these incidents in a letter to the Ministry of Transport:

> In one incident two loyal enginemen were seized and tarred, others were fired at, (one being severely wounded) whilst a large number were removed by force …and compelled by threat of violence not to convey the armed forces of the Crown or to handle munitions.[74]

Railwaymen who participated in the Munitions Strike were also subjected to intimidation. Richard Walsh, an arms agent for the IRA, gives a graphic account of the violence facing some railwaymen during the strike:

> I have seen railwaymen being hammered by police and soldiers and refusing to budge, and it was an extraordinary sight to see the detachment of military lined up on the platform fully armed and those three or four ordinary workmen getting off and telling them that they would go no further...I have seen a man of between 50 and 60 years of age, a driver, being battered and kicked around the platform by a military officer and an auxiliary officer and the revolver being put into his mouth and he still refusing to budge.[75]

Arguably the most common form of intimidation was that practiced by the companies of suspension or dismissal and loss of wages. Waterford Driver Martin White described how:

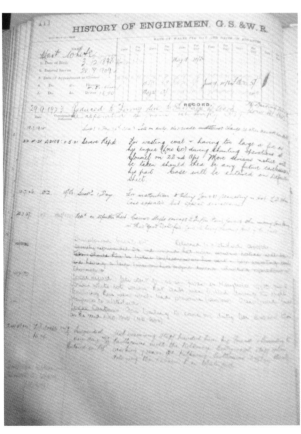

Martin White's disciplinary record. No mention of dismissal but 'severely reprimanded for waste of coal'

About 10.30 a detachment of the Devons arrived on the platform and entered my train. When starting time arrived the guard gave the green flag, but I remained stationary. I was thereupon accosted by the officer in charge accompanied by traffic inspector Hurley, who came to me and asked why I did not start. I was asked my reason for not starting the train and replied, 'I refuse to work the train while British armed forces are on board'. The inspector then instructed my fireman to uncouple the engine and informed me I was to proceed to the shed. On arrival there I was brought up in front of the district superintendent Mr. Capsey. I was dismissed for refusing to carry out my job as a driver. When the munitions strike was called off at the end of 1920 on the orders of General Michael Collins, I was reinstated, together with all the other drivers dismissed in similar circumstances.

White's dismissal was not recorded in the disciplinary record book, nor were any other dismissals in the Waterford area. Management, at least in the Waterford area, had made a conscious decision not to record Munition Strike Dismissals.

Of the five incidents of IRA intimidation on the GS&WR between June and October, the most significant was the kidnapping of the Mallow stationmaster who was 'detained' for a couple of days.[76]

He usually made it his business on such occasions to select a married man to drive although there were single men on the staff. The general feeling amongst both the public and the I.R.A. was that this was being done in order to inflict the maximum amount of hardship on the railway men concerned so it was decided to give him a bit of a shock. [77]

By November IRA Headquarters advised that kidnapping should not be undertaken without prior approval even when requested by trade union representatives, as it was damaging the cause.[78]
The majority of IRA intimidation occurred on the GNR, which differed from other companies in that the majority of its workers did not support what they perceived as a Sinn Féin initiative. Opposition would not have been confined to unionists but would also have existed among many nationalists in Ulster who supported the Irish Parliamentary Party in large numbers.

Driver O'Toole of Ennskillen explained how:

> Two men came up to me on the platform and asked me was I aware there were armed men on the train. I replied no….they say well there are and if you work them you must take the consequences. Under the circumstances I refused to work the train any further. I have been repeatedly threatened on the grounds of working military and recently had to sleep on straw half a mile away from the house in order to avoid being kidnapped. [79]

The action against driver O'Toole was part of an IRA campaign to close the Bundoran branch which served Finner military camp near Ballyshannon. The branch required three sets of drivers and fireman to operate it, and between 25 and 27 August two drivers and a fireman were kidnapped. On 28 August the last remaining driver (O'Toole) refused to go further than Ballyshannon when armed troops joined the train. The company then closed the line.[80]

The train steamed out taking the (h)armless warriors with it amid cheers of a large crowd.

Other refusals on the GNR were not as a result of direct intimidation but were based on fear of the consequences. At Gormanstown an RIC officer who was described as being 'slightly intoxicated', very publicly asked driver Coulter if he had any objection to transporting his men. It was only then that Coulter refused, saying he 'would have turned a blind eye had the officer not approached him in front of a number of people at the station'. Despite his manager making a report on the case blaming the intoxicated police officer for interfering, Coulter was dismissed.[81]

Some explanations for refusal to carry armed troops or munitions turned the railway rule book back on the company. Driver Hamill was approached on Amiens Street station platform by a group of men who warned him not to work a munitions train. When he refused he cleverly cited rule 24: 'The company's servants must not expose themselves to danger'.

It is impossible to ascertain how many of those who refused were strategically pleading intimidation. GNR management believed that fear of the consequences was being pleaded to disguise political or union motivation. 'In the great majority of cases these men have not hesitated to embarrass the company', was the view of the General Manager.[82] Those workers who claimed 'fear of the consequences' as a justification for refusal fared better on reinstatement than others. Those citing principles found their names on a file entitled 'refusal to work traffic, men NOT to be reinstated'.

The Strike in Ulster

Dismissals started in the third week of June and when rumours began to circulate that the strike would spread to the GNR, the Dublin branch officers of ASLEF went to see Tom Johnson, Secretary of Congress, to clarify the situation. Johnson told them that 'Sinn Féin would go to any length to stop the Great Northern'. The branch officers then met the head of the locomotive department and suggested that all munitions trains should be transferred to men from the Northern division. This proposal was not accepted and the first refusals on the GNR occurred on 25 June. The strike was concentrated around Dublin, Dundalk and Clones. Of the 65 dismissals of GNR locomotive crew, two-thirds were of men based in Dublin or Dundalk.[83]

In July 1920 an outbreak of sectarian violence engulfed the Lagan valley from Banbridge to Belfast. Following a speech by Sir Edward Carson there was a wave of workplace expulsions in Belfast and the surrounding districts. The victims were mainly Catholics together with a significant number of Socialists and union activists. Protestant activists were known as 'rotten prods'. The GNR did not escape this wave, and in the locomotive shed and workshop at Adelaide, near the Lisburn Road in Belfast the Catholic maintenance staff were expelled. On the other hand, a delegation of loyalists met management and explained that Catholic firemen and drivers had not been targeted because 'By driving their trains and carrying out government duty they had...proven sufficiently that they are loyal'.[84]
As the dispute spread more and more men were dismissed and to cope with the shortage of staff, the GNR closed the line from Dundalk to Enniskillen and the Carrickmacross, Cootehill branches with effect from 20 September.

The *Ulster Gazette* reported that a number of traders were considering the purchase of lorries to fill the gap in goods transport services.[85]

The company's servants must not expose themselves to danger.

The differing sentiments expressed by NUR branches in Ulster reflected the political divisions in the province and demonstrate the dilemma faced by the London leadership of the NUR. The Banbridge branch passed a resolution:

> Pledging support to the Government in handling munitions or in carrying troops; expressing disapproval of a section of Irish railwaymen who have refused to do so; and approving of the action of their delegate at the Bristol conference in not supporting the three resolutions that were adopted.

The Ballymena branch passed a resolution:

> Assuring the Prime Minister of full-hearted support in the suppression of lawlessness, plunder, treason, and murder in Ireland, and urging the Government to send still more troops, if necessary. The resolution also expressed unalterable loyalty to his Majesty the King.[86]

A very different motion was passed by the Derry branch refusing to:

> Convey or assist in the conveyance of armed military or police, to be utilised for the destruction of our fellow-countrymen. We absolutely and emphatically refuse to be parties to the creation of a second Amritzar, [87] and we pledge ourselves to support by every means in our power our colleagues who have already been suspended for advocating this principle.[88]

Operating trains of troops or munitions had both a political and a financial attraction for those opposed to the Munitions Strike. From late July extra hours worked or extra trains run due to disruption were worked at double time.[89] In addition firemen were promoted to drivers, in accordance with the number of higher duty shifts worked. The disciplinary culture was relaxed for those who worked troops or police. In July 1920 Driver Hagan of Belfast was on a disciplinary charge relating to damage to his locomotive, but was informed 'only that he had shown himself as a man willing to stand by the company he would have been fined'.[90]

In November 1920, one hundred and eleven 'Loyal Enginemen of the Belfast District' submitted a petition to the GNR Board threatening a stoppage if any reinstatement of munitions strikers took place.[91] The Board refused any dilution of their right to manage, even to delegations of the workforce with similar political views. They reserved the right to dismiss some but not all of the strikers, and that in any event they stated that the Government would have a say in who returned to work and most dismissed men would be taken back.[92]

Tensions within the Unions

The Munitions Strike exposed tensions within the unions both in Ireland and in Britain. Within the TUC, the left favoured full Irish self-determination, while the right, led by J.H. Thomas was pro-Empire and favoured Dominion Home Rule. Thomas was once described as 'liking to appear at a dinner with a trousers and coat made out of the Union Jack'.[93] This attitude made him few friends in Irish separatist circles as can be seen in the Republican magazine *New Ireland*:

> English NUR had characteristically turned traitor on its Irish members who have refused to handle munitions of war made by English workers and carried to our shores by English railwaymen to be used by other English workers against Irish workers or comrades as they are called when the NUR wanted their money and help. Such is the internationalism and 'workers solidarity' of the egregious J.H. Thomas and his associates.[94]

The fact that Thomas was at best lukewarm on Irish demands for independence might be expected to have undermined the position of the union in Ireland, especially as it was targeted by the IRB Labour Board which worked to establish Irish unions and to smash the British based unions.[95] A Labour Board member who worked in Inchicore Railway Works, stated in his Military Service Pension application that efforts to target the NUR and create an Irish Railway union failed.[96] (The NUR was to survive as a British based union in Ireland until 1952). J.H. Thomas was a skilled negotiator and perhaps his greatest achievement was delivering the eight hour day for railwaymen in February 1919. Martin O'Sullivan explained:

> The application of the eight-hour day was bitterly opposed by the government of the day and the railway companies, but they were forced to accept the demand of Mr. Thomas. So, the eight-hour day was put into operation on all our Irish lines in 1918. The Right Honourable J.H. Thomas was the best friend Irish railwaymen ever had. [97]

The original agreement shows that Ireland was not included in the eight hour day victory. The phrase 'and Ireland' was a handwritten addition to the original text. Irish railwaymen always believed that Thomas had made this amendment.[98]

The NUR did, however, lose members in this period, not due to the union's position on the strike but to the organising actions of another British based union, ASLEF. Conflict between ASLEF and NUR was brought to the attention of Michael Collins who was advised that 'the two unions were at loggerheads and always trying to steal a march on the other'.[99] Republican attempts at creating Irish based unions occasionally came across some contradictions. While the IRB Labour Board in Dublin was trying to eliminate British unions a republican activist in Cork, driver Frank Dempsey of Mallow was a leading organiser for ASLEF. Dempsey's republican credentials can be established by the fact that he took special leave to join De Valera on his American tour. [100]

'Throttling the Railways'

The British decided to defeat the strike by closing, if necessary, the entire railway system outside of Ulster. 'I am to be chairman of a committee of three to control the throttling of the Irish Railway system - the other two will be representatives of the Ministry of Transport and the military … we went down to the Castle at six and met the railway directors who at first declined to meet the Ministry of Transport or the Chief Secretary at any Government office' wrote Sturgis in his diary on 11 October. In these circumstances it is no wonder that no railway interests were appointed to this Committee.

1. The principle of an 8 hour day for all members of the wages staff has been conceded and is to come into operation on February 1st. *1919,*

2. All existing conditions of service to remain unaltered pending the decision of a Committee to be set up as soon as possible to review wages and other conditions of service of railway men in Great Britain *and Ireland*

December 1918.

J.J.Stanley
President of the Board of Trade.

The Eight Hour Day Agreement: amended to include Ireland

Hamar Greenwood told the House of Commons in late October that:

> I would rather see every railway in Ireland shut down for a hundred years than yield one inch to the claim of the Irish Republican Army that any Irish railway company subsidised by the British government should refuse to carry these loyal servants of the Crown.[101]

The absence of agreement between the Government and the railway companies as to how to handle the strike is evident in the minutes of the British Cabinet throughout the dispute. As far as they were concerned the companies were 'not obeying orders', despite the fact that they were receiving subsidies in the form of 'compensation payments', going back to an agreement made to ensure control of the railways during the War. The irony of this was not lost on Hamar Greenwood who denounced rhe absurdity of the Government continuing to subsidise, at the expense of taxpayers, the shareholders of a Railway Company that refuse to carry Government traffic.[102]

In October the government found a way to impose their policy. Eric Geddes tabled a proposal for the Cabinet meeting of 14 October which would allow the Government to order the closure of sections of railway line and to order the dismissal of munition strikers on the lines which remained open. Legislation which would allow the Government to cancel or alter any agreement with the railway companies was to be introduced. This would mean the cessation of dividend payments to shareholders. Geddes met the companies immediately before the cabinet meeting and reached an agreement that allowed them to avoid these threatened measures. The deal was that when the Government requested the closure of a section of line the company concerned would do so. In return they would maintain their subsidies.[103] The obstacles to closing the railway system outside Ulster had been removed.

Endgame

The efforts of Sturgis' committee began to bear fruit. The *Railway Gazette* reported on the 12 November that the country was within measurable distance of closing down three out of the four largest railway companies and that the MGWR would give notice of intent to close all services on 21 November. 'Things must be in a very bad way now with the railwaymen' wrote Diarmuid Fawsitt, the Sinn Féin Consul in New York to Michael Collins. 'It is obvious that the British are attempting to blockade the country, and no one regrets more than I do the delay in securing relief'.[104] The Lord Mayor of Dublin convened a national meeting of local authorities, trade unions and the IRA, on 12 November to discuss the continuation of food supplies in the event of a total railway shutdown. This involved creating an alternative food supply network using road, sea and canal transport.[105] It was planned that this network should be controlled by a national committee, similar to the one which had successfully organised the 1918 anti-conscription campaign. On the same day an order was made under the Restoration of Order in Ireland Act allowing the military to take over sections of line, 'to restrict prohibit or compel the handling of any

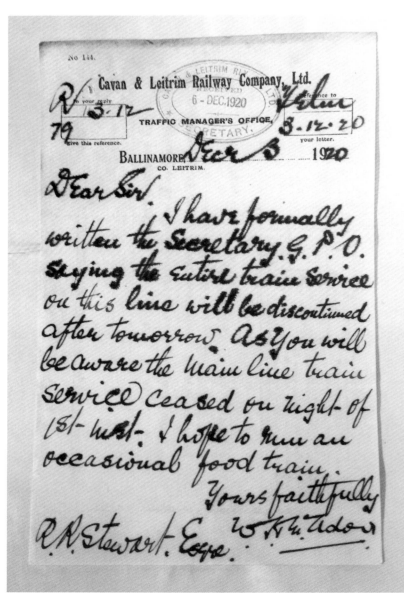

No 144.

Cavan & Leitrim Railway Company, Ltd.

6 - DEC.1920

TRAFFIC MANAGER'S OFFICE,

BALLINAMORE, Decr 3 1920
CO. LEITRIM.

Dear Sir,

I have formally written the Secretary. G. P. O. saying the entire train service on this line will be discontinued after tomorrow. As you will be aware the main line train service ceased on night of 18t inst. I hope to run an occasional food train.

Yours faithfully

R. R. Stewart. Esqre.

The Cavan & Leitrim Railway closes

particular type of traffic, and to take any necessary measures to ensure their directives were obeyed'.[106] Granting the power to take 'any necessary measures' gave the military great latitude and was a half-way house to the imposition of martial law on the railway system.

Congress held a special Conference on 14 November, at which it was decided that the railwaymen were free to change their policy but were assured that if they persisted they would receive the full support of Congress. Johnson warned that continuing the strike could put the social life of the country back a hundred years. The ultimate decision was left to the railwaymen.

In the following weeks the alternative food supply system was broken up by more intensive military repression. Many of the potential organisers of food supplies were arrested or driven underground. The proposed national committee never came into existence and local food committees were broken up by raids on union and municipal offices. Increased repression was accompanied by increased pressure by newspapers and by business interests on the railwaymen to give up their action. The views expressed in the *Dundalk Democrat* of 13 November were typical:

> The farmers will be left with the produce on their hands; traders will be left with empty shelves; the workers will go idle; and the shadow of starvation already lies over a large part of the country. "Would it not be wise, before inviting national disaster, to review the whole situation—to recognise that it is Ireland, not the British Government, that will be punished by pushing this campaign to its inevitable conclusion.

On 20 November the lines from Limerick to Waterford and Tralee were closed together with lines to Foynes, Nenagh and Killaloe. This was a prelude to wider closures and the prospect of a total shutdown of the railway system outside Ulster loomed.[107]

On 14 December the Congress executive met and concluded that:

> Changed conditions require a change of tactics, and we have decided
> to advise the Railway and Dock Workers to alter the position, and
> to offer to carry everything that the British Authorities are **willing** to
> risk on the trains.[108] (Congress emphasis)

What were these new developments? Apart from the threat to food supplies,
the months of November and December 1920 were the bloodiest months
in the struggle, with the shooting of British intelligence officers by the
IRA and the subsequent attack on Croke Park by RIC auxiliaries on 21
November and the wiping out of a unit of the RIC auxiliaries at Kilmichael
on 28 November. On 10 December, the British proclaimed martial law
in Cork, Kerry, Limerick and Tipperary. On the night of 11 December,
locomotive driver James Lawlor, coming home from work was shot by
British troops in Lismore after 'failing to respond to a challenge'.[109] RIC
auxiliaries burned Cork City on 11/12 December. This was the context in
which the Congress Executive made its decision.

NUR delegates met in Dublin on 21 December. A motion for a full
resumption of work was moved by driver Jack Kenny of Inchicore and
seconded by J. Walsh of Cork. It was passed unanimously. The railwaymen
had gone as far as they could go and decided to follow the advice of
Congress. The strike was over. J. H. Thomas wrote to Eric Geddes stating
that all traffic would be handled but that all dismissed men would have to
be reinstated. The Crown forces would regain access to the railway system.
Geddes accepted the terms of Thomas's letter.[110]

International Comparisons

When considering the options faced by Congress and the NUR it is worth
analysing two transport strikes from later in the twentieth century. The
Dutch government in exile called a railway strike in the Autumn of 1944
in anticipation of early liberation by Allied forces. The initial German
reaction was one of confusion, followed by the imposition of an embargo
on the transport of food and fuel. This precipitated a famine which lasted
almost until the end of the war in Europe. The German Commissioner Seyss
Inquart wrote: 'If the railwaymen don't return to work, a large part of the
Dutch population is threatened with starvation'.[111]

In 1949-50 French dockers refused to load arms destined for the Colonial war in Indochina, while railwaymen in Lyon, Brest, Nantes and other locations refused to work trains loaded with munitions.[112] Algerian dockers in the port of Oran had started a similar campaign six months previously. The French authorities ruthlessly suppressed these protests, with mass dismissals and the shooting of strikers. The main dockers' union, the Confederation General du Travail was described by the Prefect of Marseille as having been decapitated.[113]

The Aftermath of The Strike

A general return to work took place immediately after Christmas. Sometimes the military were surprised at the speed of resumption. Sturgis wrote of 'a story going round of the armed party who boarded a train, expecting to be back in barracks in an hour and who most unexpectedly were carried to a destination to which they had no wish to proceed where they waited some hours for a train back'. No victimization was reported on any lines except on the GNR, where the general manager demanded that every man make a personal application for reinstatement and give written guarantees as to their future behaviour. About forty men were kept out in a breach of the return to work agreement. The vindictive attitude of the GNR went further than the army, where, according to Sturgis, General Macready had told officers in charge of troops travelling that 'there was to be no crowing'.[114]

It is obvious that the British are attempting to blockade the country.

The GNR was intent on imposing uniquely draconian terms, perhaps to deter future strikes. Ten out of the sixty six locomotive staff dismissed were refused reinstatement and the issue wasn't fully resolved until March 1922.[115] It was to take another year to sort out pension and seniority issues. Each ASLEF branch passed a motion recording their approval of the reinstatement package. Many of the 'loyal enginemen of the northern district' who had signed a petition against reinstatement in November

To the Directors and other Persons concerned
with the Management of the Great Southern
and Western Railway undertaking.

In pursuance of the powers contained in the Ministry of

Transport Act 1919, and with your concurrence, the Minister

of Transport herewith directs you to discontinue the working

of, and to close all stations upon, the under-mentioned

sections of your Undertaking, in respect of traffic upon such

sections:-

              Killonan and Nenagh
              Limerick and Waterford
              Limerick and Tralee
              Ballingrane and Foynes
              Birdhill and Killaloe.

Given under the Seal of the Minister of Transport this 20th

day of November 1920.

            (sgd) G R Brooke.
                    Assistant Secretary.
LS

The Great Southern and Western Railway Company formally concurs

in the closing of the above mentioned Lines in accordance with

the undertaking signed on 12th October 1920.

            (signed)   R Crawford

                         Secretary

                      Great Southern & Western Railway Co.
Kingsbridge Terminus
      22nd November 1920.

A typical list of trains affected

1920, turned up at ASLEF branch meetings in 1922 and voted for full reinstatement of the dismissed men.[116] In the period between the end of the strike and March 1922, Congress used the money remaining in the munitions fund to grant £1400 to the victimised men.

Conclusions

Unarmed soldiers had been a common sight on trains throughout the strike. A harsher reality prevailed afterwards when the Congress phrase 'anything the British were *willing* to risk on the trains' was applied. IRA attacks on trains commenced in February 1921 and there were 25 attacks between then and the truce on 12 July. Most of these attacks were in the martial law area of Munster and in Dublin. In Drumcondra in June 1921, the IRA tried out their newly acquired Thompson sub machine gun in an attack on a troop train.[117]

> *The shadow of starvation already lies over a large part of the country.*

Since the American Civil War railways were at the centre of military theory on the deployment of troops. We have seen, how in late May, Macready had planned to suppress the rebellion by the use of mobile columns. This plan was frustrated by the strike which forced the British Army to use unreliable lorries travelling over bad roads. It was to be seven months before they regained the capacity to control the movement of their own troops in what was considered by them to be an integral part of their own country. The strike also severely undermined the legitimacy of the British state in Ireland.

> What was really under attack was the legitimacy of British rule. The railwaymen's opposition to 'the British authority which assumes governmental power in Ireland' was a notable contribution to this attack.[118]

As military historian and United States Air Force officer William Kautt put it: 'The railwaymen and dockers performed an outstanding service for the republican cause; all the more so because they were non-violent'. [119] The last word is best left to Driver Martin O Sullivan:

> *They were not firebrand patriots or idealists, they were just ordinary working men, carrying out their duties, but by their courage and unflinching stand they showed how unarmed men can defy and halt a mighty armed force.*

...he guards
...oin in

Second article

**By Martin
O'Sullivan**

...TERDAY I told how a group of Irish railway-...men—train drivers—made a stand against the ...ng of armed troops on the railways. The ...y was instant dismissal. Later, guards on the ... became involved.

...egards my own dis-..., here are the facts. ...J. Doherty, of ...e, and myself were at ...rea station and about ...es from our destina-...s we arrived at the ...e we could see a large ...ny of fully-armed ...military with ...s in charge.

...Doherty got the right of ...nal he refused to start. ...icer looked towards the ...and then he made a ...his men. Immedi-...wo soldiers and a fully-...sergeant slipped in be-...e officer as he walked ...e engine driver on his ...te and the officer asked ...ver why he refused to ...Doherty answered that ...ld not start while there ...single British soldier ...train.

...officer said to the ..."Your refusal to start ...train could have very ...consequences for you." ...y replied that he was ...d to accept them.

...is at this time that a ...change was made in the ...al orders. My driver was ...l to put his empty train ...ding and he worked the ...train back to the Loco ...the following morning. ...arrival he was imme-... dismissed. At this ...of the strike very many ...were dismissed and as ...was no driver for me I ...ismissed also.

Shared

...s at this stage that the ...train operators, seeing ...eat hardships that the ...ed drivers and their ...s were suffering, decided ...e the responsibility with ...ivers.

...ds steadfastly refused ...the green flag right of

...way signal to the driver. Signalmen refused to put the signals in the starting position and were dismissed, and the station staffs refused to handle British military stores or equipment of any kind, and members of many other grades were dismissed every day. And it must be repeated here that none of those men could get any strike pay, in fact very many of them got nothing either from the Collection fund. At this stage the railway authorities issued a statement that they could no longer operate their full timetables, and warning the public that they might be compelled to a further reduction of the train services owing to "The Munitions Strike."

The drivers that took part in this strike have all by now passed away, but every single one of them is entitled to have his name mentioned for their gallant stand in the Munitions Strike of 1920.

Ordinary

They were not firebrand patriots or idealists, they were just ordinary men carrying out their working duties, but by their courage and unflinching stand they showed how unarmed men can defy and halt a mighty armed force. As I have already stated those grand "old timers" are all gone but their sons and grandsons have the example they set to live up to. I have also seen many of those dismissed drivers struggling into Athlone, their headquarters, without a sole to their boots having had to walk about 100 miles to their homes as a result of the Railway Directors infamous order "Instant dismissal and on the spot."

The strike dragged on, months passed, dismissals taking place every day as the

military authorities tried every means to break the resistance of the railway men, but they failed. Meetings were frequently held by various important bodies to bring the strike to an end, but all their efforts, as the men still refused to work any train with British armed soldiers on board, came to nothing and the railway authorities stubbornly refused to reinstate them.

At last a ray of hope appears through the clouds.

The Right Honourable J. H. Thomas, Cabinet Minister in the British Government, an engine driver himself, he had risen from the footplate to one of the highest positions in his own country.

Early in December 1920 he came over and addressed a huge meeting in the Mansion House, Dublin.

Meeting

In an impassioned speech on behalf of the dismissed railwaymen he told the Irish railway authorities that if they did not reinstate them unconditionally all trade between Ireland and England would cease forthwith. The result of the meeting, the Company agreed to reinstate the men. It was a great personal victory for Mr. Thomas, this great and noblehearted Englishman, who had earlier in 1918, when he stood in the British House of Commons and threatened to resign if the eight-hour day did not apply to the railways of Ireland. The application of the eight-hour day to the Irish railways was bitterly opposed by the Government, of that time and the Railway Company, but they were forced to accept the demands of Mr. Thomas. So the eight-hour day was put into operation on all our Irish lines in 1918.

The Right Honourable J. H. Thomas was the greatest friend Irish railways ever had.

It is almost impossible to believe that those important events were not recorded in any recent history of Ireland in the years 1920 and onwards to the present day.

CONCLUDED

Payments from the Munitions of War Fund

The largest single payment went to the NUR branch in North Wall where 400 dockers were on strike, followed by a payment to Limerick Trades Council. Rosslare NUR was next, where like North Wall, the entire dock workforce was on strike. This was followed by Waterford where £10,000 was divided equally between the NUR and ASLEF. Lower levels of strike activity on the GNR can be seen by the lower amounts paid out in Ulster. Belfast received £374, slightly ahead of Dunmanway, a village in West Cork which received £366: similarly Enniskillen received only £72.50, slightly less than Ennistymon on the West Clare Railway which received £76.

LOCATION	UNION	AMOUNT PAID
North Wall*	NUR	£35,862
Limerick	Trades Council	£16,525
Rosslare Harbour	NUR	£10,588
Waterford	ASLEF	£ 5,001
Waterford	NUR	£ 4,991
Kingsbridge*	NUR	£ 4,916
Athlone	NUR	£ 2,576
Cork	NUR 3	£ 2,443
Inchicore*	NUR	£ 1,799
Derry	NUR 2	£ 1.747
Ennis	NUR	£ 1,657
Tralee	NUR	£ 1,587
Wexford	NUR	£ 1,456
Mallow	NUR	£ 1,377
Dundalk	ASLEF	£ 1,368
Broadstone*	NUR 1	£ 1,280
Amiens St*	ASLEF	£ 1,275
Cork	NUR 2	£ 1,129
Clonmel	Trades Council	£ 1,111
Ballybrophy	NUR 25%	£ 1,104
Cork	ASLEF	£ 1,074
Letterkenny	NUR	£ 1,070
Dundalk	NUR	£ 934
Cavan	NUR	£ 865
Tralee	ASLEF	£ 708
Sligo	NUR	£ 638
Kilkenny	NUR	£ 628
Amiens St*	NUR	£ 586
Drogheda	NUR	£ 541
Clones	ASLEF	£ 490
Burtonport	NUR	£ 462
Clones	NUR	£ 430
Belfast	NUR	£ 374

LOCATION	UNION	AMOUNT PAID
Broadstone*	ASLEF	£ 371
Dunmanway	NUR	£ 366
Castleblaney	NUR	£ 363
Westland Row*	NUR	£ 316
Inchicore*	ASLEF	£ 315
Tuam	NUR	£ 313
Bray	NUR	£ 301
Mullingar	NUR	£ 301
Mallow	ASLEF	£ 296
Athenry	NUR	£ 294
Galway	NUR	£ 271
Thurles	NUR	£ 228
Drogheda	ASLEF	£ 179
Broadstone*	NUR 2	£ 162
Strabane	NUR	£ 131
Bandon	NUR	£ 122
Kildare	NUR	£ 118
Derry	NUR 1	£ 117
Clara	NUR	£ 10
Newry	ASLEF	£ 106
Ballybofey	NUR	£ 94
Ennis	Ennis Labour Union	£ 92
Maryborough	NUR	£ 91
Dublin	ITGWU 1	£ 79
Newtownbutler	NUR	£ 79
Kilfree	NUR	£ 77
Ennistymon	NUR	£ 76
Enniskillen	NUR	£ 72
Derry	ASLEF	£ 66
Dunleary	NUR	£ 66
Castlebar	NUR	£ 64
Pallas	NUR	£ 61
Cobh	ITGWU	£ 59
Ballyshannon	NUR	£ 50
Killarney	NUR	£ 50
Armagh	NUR	£ 42
Fermoy	NUR	£ 40
Inchicore*	ITGWU	£ 36
Claremorris	NUR	£ 31
Dublin,	Unattached	£ 30
Grand Canal St*	NUR	£ 28
Tuam	Auto Drivers	£ 25
Terenure	ITGWU	£ 21
Tralee	RCA	£ 19
Tuam	NUR	£ 18
Westport	NUR	£ 16
Omagh	NUR	£ 15
Collooney	NUR	£ 13
Cahir	ASLEF	£ 10
Cork	Auto Drivers	£ 10
Wexford	ITGWU	£ 7
Cork	Docker's Union	£ 5
Glanworth	NUR	£ 5

Dubin based locations

SOURCES

Archives

Irish Railway Record Society Archives
Great Southern and Western Railway secretary office papers
Great Northern Railway locomotive engineer papers
Cavan and Leitrim Railway general, Manager file
Military Archives (online)
Bureau of Military History
Military Service pension Applications
Digital repository Ireland, Dáil Éireann papers DE series
National Archives UK Cabinet Minutes series CAB 23, CAB 24 available online

Publications

Derby Advertiser
Railway Gazette
National and regional press as cited in footnotes from Irish Times online and Irish Newspaper Archives
Thom's Directory Dublin, 1922
Mercantile Navy list and Maritime Directory 1920
Hansard

Books and Theses

Bullock, Alan *Ernest Bevin* vol.1 (London, 1969).
Hopkinson, Michael *The last Days of Dublin Castle* (Dublin, 1999).
Kautt, William, *Ambushes and armour* (Dublin, 2010).
Middlemas, Keith, *Tom Jones Diary* vol. 3 pp. 19-20.
Mitchell, Art, *Labour in Irish politics* (Dublin, 1974).
Morrison, Eve, *The Irish railway embargo of 1920 and the republican movement* (B.A. Dissertation. TCD 2003).
Neligan, David, *Spy in the Castle* (Dublin, 1976).
Ruscio, Alain, *Les communistes et l'Algérie: Des origins de la guerre d'indépendence*, 1920-1962, Paris, (2019).
O'Brien, William, *Forth the Banners Go* (Dublin, 1969).
Crowley, John, Ó'Drisceoil, Donal, and Murphy, Mike, *Atlas of the Irish Revolution* (Cork, 2018).

Van der Zee, Henri, *The Hunger Winter* (Lincoln, 1992).
Yeates, Pádraig, *A City in Turmoil* (Dublin, 2012).
Yeates, Padraig, *Irish craftworkers in time of revolution* (Dublin, 2016).

Articles

Howell, David, 'I loved my Union and my Country- Jimmy Thomas and the Politics of Railway Trade Unionism' *Twentieth Century British History* vol.6 no. 2 1995.
McCabe, Conor, 'A situation of great novelty and difficulty – The 1920 Irish Railway Munitions Strike', *Saothar* 45, 2020.
Macfarlane, L.J, 'Hands off Russia: Labour and the Russo-Polish War, 1920, *Past & Present*, Dec., 1967, No. 38.
O Sullivan, Martin, *Irish Independent*, August 12 and 13 1967.
Rigney, Peter, 'Military service and Railway Staff 1914 to 1923' *IRRS Journal*, vol.7 no.30, spring 2006.
Townshend, Charles, The Irish Railway Strike of 1920: Industrial Action and Civil Resistance in the Struggle for Independence' *Irish Historical Studies*, Vol. 22, No. 83 (Mar. 1979).
White, Martin, 'Recollections of Rosslare'. *IRRS Journal*, vol.7 no.30, spring 1963.

BIBLIOGRAPHY

[1] ILP&TUC *Annual Report*, 1921 refers to 1,500 dismissals .

[2] Art Mitchell, *Labour in Irish Politics*, (Dublin, 1974), p.120.

[3] Martin O' Sullivan, 'How Railwaymen Defied an Empire' *Irish Independent*, August 12/13, 1967.

[4] Charles Townshend, 'The Irish Railway Strike of 1920: Industrial Action and Civil Resistance in the Struggle for Independence' *Irish Historical Studies*, Vol. 22, No. 83 (Mar. 1979), pp. 265-282.m

[5] Ronan Fanning, *Fatal Path*, (London, 2013), p.228.

[6] Michael Hopkinson, The Last Days of Dublin Castle, (Dublin, 1999) hereafter *Sturgis Diary*, p.3.

[7] Fanning, *Fatal Path*, p.222.

[8] British National Archives, Cabinet Minutes,11 August 1920. CAB 23 series.

[9] Pádraig Yeates, *A City in Turmoil*, (Dublin 2012), p.110.

[10] Cabinet Minutes, June to Dec. 1920, CAB 23 series.

[11] Quoted in L.J. Macfarlane. 'Hands off Russia: British Labour and the Russo-Polish War, 1920' *Past & Present*, Dec. 1967, No. 38, pp. 126-146.

[12] Alan Bullock, *Ernest Bevin*, Vol.1 (London, 1960) p.134.

[13] *Derby Advertiser*, 28 May 1920 gives an account of this meeting.

[14] *Freeman's Journal*, 17 May 1920.

[15] ILP&TUC *Annual Report*, 1920, pp.34-37 for an account of the strike.

[16] ILP&TUC *Annual Report*, 1920, p. 36.

[17] Frank Robbins witness statement WS 585, pp. 154-155; Tom Johnston WS 1755, p.13.

[18] William O' Brien, *Forth the Banners Go*, (Dublin, 1969), pp.194-196.

[19] *Irish Independent*, 4 June 1920.

[20] The Bureau of Military History was established in 1947 and collected statements from those involved in the 1916 to 1921 period.

[21] The ship was an unarmed merchant ship.

[22] WS 1438 Christopher Moran, pp.11-13.

[23] IRRS Archive, GS&WR 3375, Burgess to Railway Companies, 21 April 1920.

[24] ILP&TUC *Annual Report*, 1920, p46

[25] GS&WR 3393,report to Board, 28 May & 3 June 1920.

[26] GS&WR 3393, report to Board, General Manager's Correspondence Index vol. 47.

[27] Cabinet Minutes, 31 May 1920, CAB 23 series.

[28] Keith Middlemas, *Whitehall Diary- by Thomas Jones* (London, 1969), pp. 19-20.

[29] Irish Command, *Record of the Rebellion* Vol. IV, p. 16, Quoted in William Kautt *Ambushes and Armour*, (Dublin 2010), p.61.

[30] *Railway Gazette*, 12 June 1920.

[31] G.W. Alcock, *Fifty Years of Railway Trade Unionism*, (London, 1922), p.566.

[32] *Irish Independent*, 5 June 1920.

[33] Alcock, *Fifty Years*, p.567.

[34] LE 20/2225 Statement of fireman Grey, fireman Downey.

[35] Alcock, *Fifty Years*,pp.569-570.

[36] Memorandum for Cabinet 4 December 1920, p.3, CAB 24 series; GS&WR 3393, summary of dispute.

[37] GS&WR 3393, summary of dispute.

[38] ILP&TUC *Annual Report*, 1920, page 42 & 1921, pp. 35 -41 for a narrative of the fund's establishment and pp. 68-71 for the audited accounts.

[39] www.moneysorter.co.uk

[40] Morrison, *Railway Embargo*, p.33.

[41] O' Brien, *Forth the Banners Go*, p.196.

[42] GS&WR 3393, Goulding to Bonar Law 29 June 1920

[43] ILP&TUC *Annual Report,*1920 p. 43-45.

[44] Middlemas, *Whitehall Diary*, p.32.

[45] GS&WR 3393, Maj. Gen. Rycroft to E.A Neale, 27 July 1920.

[46] *Irish Independent*, 31 July 1920.

[47] GS&WR 3393, Neale to General Managers, 28 July 1920.

[48] WS 445 Jim Slattery, p.9.

[49] David Neligan, *Spy in the Castle*, (Dublin, 1976) p.76, also Neligan WS 380, p.6.

[50] DSER file 1516

[51] WS 638, Patrick Caldwell, p.25.

[52] WS 907, Laurence Nugent, P.197. Zigman cigarette manufacturers was at 7 Lr. Baggot Street. *Thom's Directory*, 1922, p.1828.

[53] Cabinet Minutes 11 Aug. 1920, CAB/23 series.

[54] *Sturgis Diary*, p.34, 19 Aug.

[55] GS&WR 3393, Marwood to Goulding, 27 August 1920.

[56] Freeman's Journal, 31 Aug. 1920.

[57] Ibid.

[58] GNR 20/2225 Bagwell to Glover 14 Oct.1920

[59] *Sturgis Diary*, p. 55.

[59] WS 1099, G.C. Duggan, p.29.

[60] ILP&TUC *Annual Report*, 1921, p.6.

[61] GS&WR 3393, Report to board, 19 Aug. 1920.

[62] *Belfast Newsletter*, 28 June 1920.

[63] *Southern Star*, 17 July 1920.

[64] *Southern Star*, 25 Sept. 1920.

[65] WS 413, Pat McCrea, p.11: Freeman's Journal 20 July 1920.

[66] *Belfast Newsletter*, 30 July 1920.

[67] *Belfast Newsletter,* 10 Aug. 1920.

[68] WS 951 Robert Knightly, p.1. GS&WR file 3393.

[69] C&LR file, IRRS archives.

[70] Peter Rigney 'Military service and railway staff' *IRRS Journal*, vol.22 no.161, September 2006, p.263.

[71] *Anglo Celt*, 24 July 1920.

[72] Townshend, '*Irish Railway Strike*', p.280.

[73] Eve Morrison, *The Irish Railway Embargo of 1920 and the Republican Movement BA Thesis*, TCD), 2003, Appendix B.

[74] GSWR 3393, Goulding to Ministry of Transport London, 18 Aug. 1920.

[75] WS 400, Richard Walsh, p.144.

[76] Morrison, *Railway Embargo*, Appendix B.

[77] WS 1036, John Moloney p.5.

[78] National Library of Ireland, Thomas Johnson Papers, MS 17,134/3.

[79] IRRS Archive, GNR Locomotive Engineer's File, LE 20/2225.

[80] *Belfast Newsletter*, 30 Aug. 1920.

[81] These statements are all in file GNR LE 20/2225

[82] GNR LE 20/2225, Bagwell to Glover, 14 Oct. 1920.

[83] GNR LE 20/2225, Minute of meeting, list of dismissed men.

[84] GNR LE/2972, 'Belfast disturbances -requests by staff for police protection' Undated minute of meeting of GNR in Adelaide depot.

[85] Des Fitzgerald, *The GNR and the IRA*, (unpublished typescript) p. 43.

[86] *Belfast Newsletter*, 28 June 1920.

[87] Amritsar is a Sikh holy city in northern India where on 13 April 1919 troops under the command of General Dyer fired on a crowd of demonstrators killing at least 379 people.

[88] *Belfast Newsletter*,30 July 1920.

[89] GNR LE 20/2225, Deniss to Glover 17 July 1920.

[90] IRRS Archive, GNR Enginemens' Record book, p.28.

[91] GNR LE 20/2225 E contains this petition.

[92] GNR Board Minute 25 Jan. 1921.

[93] David Howell, 'I Loved my Union and my Country: -Jimmy Thomas and the Politics of Railway Trade Unionism' *Twentieth Century British History* vol.6 no. 2 1995, pp. 146-173.

[94] *New Ireland*, 19 June 1920.

[95] Pádraig Yeates, *Irish craftworkers in time of revolution*, (Dublin, 2016) describes this process.

[96] MSP 21793, John J. Rooney, sworn typescript statement p.3: Rooney was a coachmaker in Inchicore.

[97] O' Sullivan 'Railwaymen defied an Empire'.

[98] Conversation with the late driver Paddy Guilfoyle, Inchicore.,1979.

[99] NAI Dáil Éireann papers DE 2/48, Art O Briain to Collins 14 Feb. 1921.

[100] GS&WR 3454 'Request of driver Dempsey for special leave'.

[101] *Railway Gazette*, 20 Oct. 1920.

[102] Cabinet Minutes 11 Aug 1920, CAB/23 series.

[103] Geddes Memorandum for Cabinet, 4 Dec. 1920, CAB/24 series.

[104] NAI Dáil Éireann papers DE 2/48 Fawsitt to Collins 14 Nov. 1920.

[105] DE 2/48 Boland to Collins, 14 Nov. 1920; Dáil memo 'Arrangements made for provisioning of the city' 15 November 1920.

[106] Geddes Memorandum for Cabinet, 4 Dec. 1920, CAB 24 series.

[107] GS&WR 3393, copy of closure order.

[108] ILP&TUC 1921 *Annual Report*, p.10.

[109] *Irish Examiner*, 13 December 1920.

[110] *Railway Gazette*, 30 December 1920 reproduces the correspondence.

[111] Henri van der Zee, *The Hunger Winter*, (Lincoln 1992), p.31.

[112] Assemblé Nationale Francaise, 17 May 1951, p.5635.

[113] Ruscio, Alain, *Les communistes et l'Algérie: Des origins á ka guerre d'indepéndence*, 1920-1962, Paris, (2019).

[114] *Sturgis Diary*, p.98.

[115] LE 20/2225A, memo 24 Jan. 1921.

[116] LE 20/2225C 'Refusal to work traffic': Glover to Dennis, 2 March 1923. Greene to Glover 20 Feb. 1921, Squance ASLEF to Glover 26 Feb 1921.

[117] Ian Cantwell,y '*Attacks on Troop Trains 1921*'at https://independent. academia.edu/IanCantwell/website-article

[118] Townshend, *Railway Strike*, p.282.

[119] Kautt, *Ambushes and Armour*, p.60.